Cyber Citizenship and Cyber Safety™

Viruses and Spam

Deirdre Day-MacLeod

rosen publishing's
rosen central®

New York

For Rory and Sinead, who will grow up in the Information Age

Published in 2008 by The Rosen Publishing Group, Inc.
29 East 21st Street, New York, NY 10010

Library of Congress Cataloging-in-Publication Data

Day-MacLeod, Deirdre.
Viruses and spam / Deirdre Day-MacLeod.—1st ed.
    p. cm.—(Cyber citizenship and cyber safety)
Includes bibliographical references and index.
ISBN-13: 978-1-4042-1351-7 (lib. bdg.)
1. Computer security. 2. Computer crimes. 3. Cyberterrorism. I. Title.
QA76.9.A25 D395 2008
005.8—dc22

2007029654

Manufactured in Malaysia

Contents

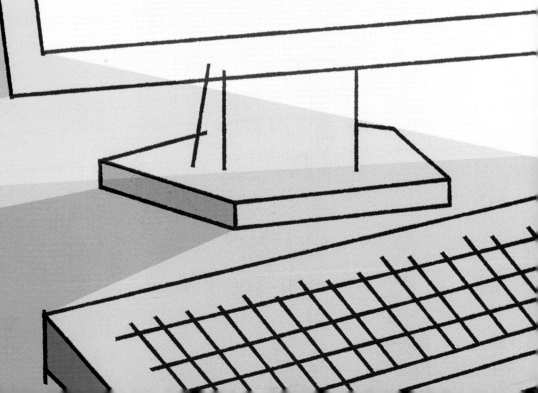

Introduction

Could a computer virus alter the results of a presidential election? Could a hacker change all of the traffic lights at a given moment so that accidents would occur simultaneously at intersections across the country? While there might be some debate about the probability of either event, the fact is that both are possible. From the computers at NASA to those of the government of Estonia, computer systems across the world have suffered attacks from unknown hackers whose spam and viruses have spread havoc and confusion, not to mention cost millions of dollars to repair.

The criminals of the twenty-first century use modems and mice and change e-mail addresses rather than speed off in getaway cars. How we stop cyber criminals is still an

Gary McKinnon, who was accused of hacking into American military Web sites and breaching security, is fighting to remain in England rather than face trial in the United States.

open question and one that is being debated even as this book is written. In the time between when these words left the computer they were written upon and when they were electronically transmitted to editor, proofreader, and printer, new viruses and antivirus programs were developed. Criminals were brought to justice and others disappeared.

The more we depend upon computers, the more we need to know about computer safety. This book is a place to start learning about these threats, but like all things computerized, spam and viruses are continually and rapidly changing. Once you close this book, open your browser and find out what is happening right now.

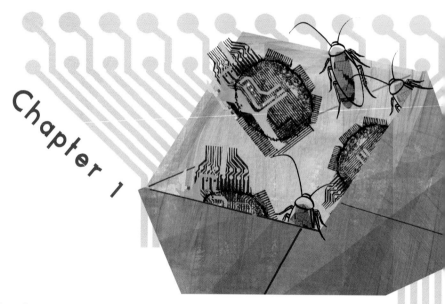

Catching Viruses and Suffering from Spam

It would take a long time to list all of the ways that the Internet influences how we live our lives. In the Information Age, all you need is a computer and an Internet connection to send e-mail and instant messages. You can hunt down facts or post your feelings on a blog. You can put a video up on YouTube and your photos on Flickr. It's easy to make contact with people anywhere in the world who share your interests. You can read their blogs, look at their videos and their photographs, and then express your feelings about them. You can download music, videos, photographs, and games.

Even the simplest tasks, like getting directions and movie start times, are ones we routinely perform online. It's hard to believe that not so long ago a person would have had to use books, maps, newspapers, and telephones to do the things we now do without leaving our desks.

There is no doubt that the wired world of the Web has made life better for most of us. Along with all of the good things, however, there are some not so great things. These may be simply annoying, expensive, time consuming, or down-right dangerous. You've read about the amazing discoveries of the first explorers from Europe when they came to the New World of the Americas. And though they found great riches and encountered new animals and communities of people, they brought with them diseases that killed thousands and thousands of natives.

The Internet allows you to have access to everything from scientific documents and newspapers to games and chat rooms.

Or, in a smaller and far less dramatic way, you might have noticed how easy it is to catch a cold when one of your classmates starts sneezing. Contact with other people may be enlightening and exciting, but it brings with it some dangers to consider as well.

Computer viruses and spam are the darker side of all of the technological advances we now enjoy. Many people lump

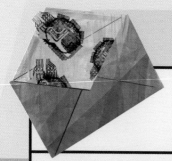

Three Ways to Catch a Virus

- The virus infects files on a system shared by a network of computers.

- The virus travels from one computer to another when using floppy disks or other removable storage.

- An infected file is attached to an e-mail and opened by the computer user.

viruses, worms, spam, spyware, and all of the various programs that are harmful to our computers into the category of "malware."

If you never used the Internet, e-mail, instant messages, chat rooms, or computer disks or played CDs and DVDs on your computer, then you would never have had the chance of infecting your computer with malware. However, being this cautious with your computer would be like staying home all winter and refusing to see anyone in order to avoid a cold. Not only is it not so much fun, it's not very practical.

As you probably guessed, the word "virus" itself comes from biology. Like diseases that jump from person to person through contact, viruses spread from computer to computer through various forms of interaction. Computers that have viruses are said to be "infected." A virus can spread through a network of computers and from there to more and more computers in an amazingly short time.

A computer virus is a program that can copy itself and infect a computer without the user even knowing about it. A virus actually works its way into a network file system—the set of rules, or protocols, that govern how the computer works.

Every time you transfer files to your computer—whether by disk or via the Internet—you risk potential infection.

Once a virus has infected a computer, it can re-create itself (sort of like how a biological virus re-creates itself) and spread through the entire system. Some viruses are programmed to hurt your computer by damaging programs, deleting files, or reformatting your hard disk. They may also plant text, images, or audio messages on your computer. Even those viruses that are called "benign," meaning they aren't deliberately trying to do any damage, take up space in your computer and cause programs to malfunction or stop working.

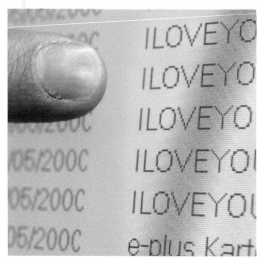

An e-mail box seemingly filled with loving messages actually contains far less charming content: the ILOVEYOU virus.

No one can tell how many viruses are alive on the Internet right now. While computer scientists create antivirus software, hackers continue to create new viruses that bypass the latest technology. Sometimes hackers make antivirus viruses or become the people helping to safeguard computers.

As nasty as viruses are, even more common and more costly is spam.

Spam is the e-mail version of junk mail that clutters our real-world mailboxes. Because it is far cheaper and easier to create and send than paper mail, you'll find spam everywhere. Bulk e-mails clutter in-boxes with offers of free money, cures for illnesses, or cheap products. Spam also intrudes in instant messages, newsgroups, search engines, blogs, cell phones, and pretty much any place else spammers can find a way in.

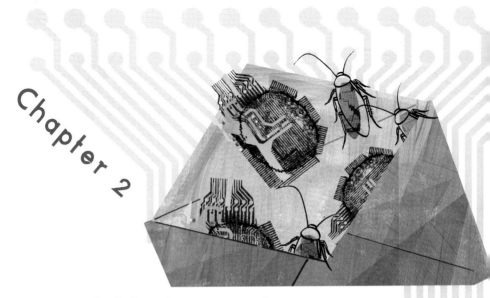

Chapter 2

A Short History of Viruses and Spam

The Internet Crime Complaint Center is run by the Federal Bureau of Investigation (FBI) and the National White Collar Crime Center. The Internet Crime Complaint Center estimates that financial losses from viruses and spam reached $183 million in 2005. A *Consumer Reports* survey found that viruses, spyware, and spam had cost computer users as much as $7.8 billion in just two years. These are pretty amazing numbers when you consider that fifteen years ago very few people were conscious that such malicious software existed at all. And even some of the most computer-savvy people believed that viruses were myths. One prominent computer expert even suggested that spam was like the alligators that many imagined to live in the New York City sewers. While most (if not all) of us don't have to worry about the monstrous

In May 2000, FBI agent Rubin Garcia and Attorney General Janet Reno announced the creation of the Internet Fraud Complaint Center, a partnership between the FBI and the National White Collar Crime Center.

offspring of poorly chosen pets, there are few e-mailers who haven't confronted the menace of spam.

The Dawn of Computers

The first uses of self-reproducing and malicious code (in other words, viruses) appeared sometime between the 1950s and 1960s in the laboratories of universities and government organizations. A group of programmers engaged in a contest called Core Wars, which involved players trying to write code that could replicate (copy) itself as quickly as possible. (In those days "core" had been used to describe a computer's memory.) Instead of playing against each other, the contestants were creating the players in the game.

The Creeper virus challenged users, but it never left the network where it was first created. The Creeper spread only through computers within its own network. Eventually someone created the Reeper virus, which destroyed the Creeper. To this day no one knows who created either program.

Elk Cloner

In the early 1980s, ninth-grader Rich Skrenta created Elk Cloner, the first virus to appear "in the wild," or beyond the lab or the computer where it was created. Skrenta put his virus on floppy disks, removable disks upon which people store and exchange programs and other files. Since there were no networks then, the only way to move information from one computer to another was physically on these floppies. Skrenta realized that he could give his classmates disks with games on them but that he could hide his virus alongside the game. Skrenta claims his virus was a practical joke and a "hack." Today Skrenta runs a blog where he wrote that "the essence of the hack isn't just realizing you can use a system in a new, unexpected way. It's getting a disproportionate effect from your effort."

Trojan Horses

In 1983, Fred Cohen, a doctoral student in computer science, wrote a dissertation naming the self-perpetuating programs that had begun to spring up "viruses." "Trojan horses" had begun to appear. These programs act like the device the ancient Greeks used to lay siege to the city of Troy. (One morning the Trojans awakened to find no Greek armies surrounding their city, but in their place stood a huge wooden horse. Believing that this horse was a gift and that the Greeks had given up, the Trojans dragged the horse into the center of their city. That night as they slept, Greek soldiers emerged from a trapdoor in the belly of the horse, taking the sleeping Trojans by surprise.) Trojan Horse viruses therefore appear as gifts but contain something else that is not so welcome.

The New Generation

By the late 1980s, viruses began spreading all over the world even though most people didn't take them seriously. Peter Norton, a computer guru, even announced publicly that computer viruses were a myth, like the alligators in New York City sewers. (Ironically, Norton sold his company, Norton

David L. Smith, the creator of the Melissa virus, caused millions of dollars of damage and was one of the first people sentenced for committing a cyber crime.

Antivirus, to another computer company called Symantec, which released some of the most popular antivirus software.)

As antivirus programs were developed, viruses, in response, became trickier and more complicated. Hackers saw each development in antivirus technology as a challenge. Soon there were stealth viruses, which were nearly impossible to find, and polymorphic viruses, which could change, or "morph," once they had loaded themselves onto a computer.

Then there were the viral hoaxes and exaggerations, which caused as much damage as real viruses. The Michelangelo virus was designed to unleash a digital apocalypse on March 6, painter Michelangelo's birthday. The e-mail warning of a virus named Good Times caused panic and disruption. Neither virus actually existed.

By the end of the twentieth century, viruses had become commonplace in Windows and other Microsoft products and were growing increasingly more complex and difficult to detect, remove, and recover from. The Melissa virus, for instance, would occupy a computer and then forward itself to fifty people in the owner's e-mail address book. In this way it spread faster than any virus ever. The Chernobyl virus rendered hard drives impossible to access, and Bubbleboy was the first worm to activate when the user opened an e-mail message in the e-mail software Outlook.

The New Millennium

In 2000, the VBS/Loveletter virus with the subject line "ILOVEYOU" appeared and caused $10 billion in damage. Clever hackers had realized that people will readily open e-mails that speak of love.

You might call 2001 the Year of the Worm. Ranub, Simile, Sadmind, Sircam, Code Red, Code Red II, Nimda, and Klez were worms that all made their first appearances in that year.

Hackers were learning to use false e-mail addresses so that their viruses would appear to come from addresses that were either faked or pulled from the address book of an infected machine. The Sobig worm appeared to come from the e-mail address big@boss.com and caused $29.7 billion of damage worldwide. Mass-mailed viruses could spread with incredible speed, moving quickly from one computer to another. Within hours, thousands of computers would become compromised.

In late 2006 and early 2007, two worms made their first appearance on the social networking site MySpace. One would visit profiles and change all the names of a person's contacts to "lOrdOfthenOOse." Another worm made it appear as if all of a person's friends were named EricAndrew. It was estimated that 70 percent of all MySpace profiles, over 70 million, were infected.

Since the time of limited networks in labs and floppy disks, viruses have spread through millions of computers all over the world. The Internet increased the speed of infection. Today viruses are spread on CDs or embedded in programs or even hard drives before they are sold to unsuspecting shoppers. Viruses travel fastest via the Internet and e-mail, sometimes spreading through thousands and thousands of computers within hours. Some viruses begin in one place and as the day

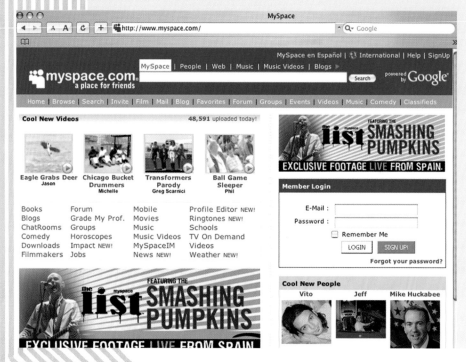

MySpace users became the targets of fraud when music download sites they believed they had been referred to by friends were used to steal financial information from them.

wears on and people wake up and power up their machines, they spread from country to country as if they were following the sun.

Since each infected computer infects more computers, the numbers grow so fast that unless the virus is stopped, it could theoretically infect every computer in the world in a matter

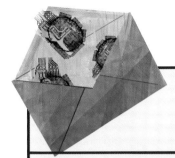

Where Spam Got Its Name

The name "spam" arises from a method that members of Internet chat rooms used to get rid of unwelcome visitors. In the late 1970s, reruns of *The Monty Python Show* continually played a skit about a restaurant that served only the luncheon meat Spam. The skit ended with a chorus of Vikings singing the word "spam" over and over. For some reason, the regular users of certain online bulletin boards began to type the script to this skit whenever a stranger entered their conversations.

While the script occupied all of the screen space nothing else could be typed. Eventually the strangers gave up, the chatters returned to their regular conversations, and "spam" became a name for unwelcome visitors to the Internet, much like the e-mails that clog one's mailbox.

of weeks. Viruses could disrupt everything from mail delivery to presidential elections. Viruses that appeared a decade or more ago are still alive, even if they aren't as common as their more sophisticated descendants.

In a world where we have become dependent upon our Internet connections for such daily tasks as shopping and research, it boggles the mind to consider what damage can be wrought by viruses. Even more amazing is the idea that the next supervirus could be created as easily by a high school student as it could by a computer scientist.

Spam

Unlike viruses, which are often created simply for fun or by computer programmers who want to demonstrate flaws in programs, spam is usually all about the money. Spammers may send out their messages purely to engage in deliberate fraud. Spammers often use false names, addresses, phone numbers, and other contact information to set up "disposable" e-mail accounts at various Internet service providers. Spammers might want to sell you some magical weight-loss cure or convince you to send money to someone overseas on false pretenses.

Spam is often used to collect personal information, which is then sold to data companies. At its worst, spammers engage in identity theft, meaning they try to take your personal information in order to get credit cards or loans, and make purchases in your name. Spam can install viruses and spyware on your computer or simply suck up disk space.

Like the creators of viruses, the people who make spam have become trickier and more sophisticated as time has passed.

Fighting Viruses and Spam

As quickly as viruses and spam change, so must the ways we protect ourselves against them. Computer viruses have ways of developing their own protections and becoming sneakier and more devious.

There are easy ways to keep yourself and your computer safe. You should always take measures to prevent attacks. Just as the ancient kings built castles with high walls and took care to let the gangplank down only for selected visitors, computer users have to guard against enemies. This means using firewalls and antivirus software.

You should also protect your computer's health by simply paying attention to it and taking immediate action when you sense something is wrong. Notice when files suddenly aren't working properly, or when your computer seems a bit sluggish or begins doing odd things. Once you realize that your security has been breached, you have to find a way to handle the problems and clean up your machine.

Remember it is more than likely that you will at some point need to fix a problem. There have been estimates that 90 percent of all computers are carrying, have carried, or will carry viruses. And it might not be too crazy to suggest that we all have received spam.

Protection and Prevention

Use a firewall and antivirus software. Your computer probably has a firewall built in, but you need to make sure it is activated. A firewall's function is like the special walls used in construction that are designed to keep fires from spreading through the entire building.

When you run virus software, you usually can get updates and reminders. Since new viruses are popping up all the time, your protection needs to keep pace. You can usually download "patches," which will protect you as soon as the latest viruses are on the loose. Install any security updates or patches for your operating system promptly.

Likewise, to protect yourself from spam, you have to be careful. You can't just open any e-mail that pops in your in-box. And even if an e-mail comes from a familiar address, never

There are a host of antivirus products and numerous approaches to the challenge of protecting computers from viruses.

open an attachment unless you are absolutely certain that it is safe.

Don't leave your e-mail address at any sites you aren't sure of. Spammers have programs called spambots, which scan Web sites and Usenet logs for e-mail addresses. Submit e-mail addresses only to sites that you trust and respect.

Many Internet providers offer virus protection, spyware, and spam protection programs along with their other services.

Choose your e-mail address wisely. Spammers generate addresses that seem likely to exist. If you have an obvious name, you are setting yourself up for an attack.

Be careful when opening e-mail attachments. (It merits repeating.) You can usually set your mail server to ask you before it downloads any attachments and images.

If you receive an attachment you aren't expecting, do not open it. Before you open any e-mail attachment—even if it's from someone you trust—scan it using antivirus software. Many programs such as Yahoo! Mail automatically scan all e-mail attachments for viruses.

Back Up Your Files

Have your data saved on some kind of removable media like a disk or other backup drive

With an external hard drive you can back up all your files so that they are safe if your computer suffers from an attack or some other misfortune.

in case your computer is compromised by a virus. Make this a regular part of your life, like using a seatbelt or wearing a bike helmet.

You can also use an automated antispam system to stop spam from getting into your in-box. These systems and services either block or filter spam. Blocking means rejecting any mail that comes from likely spamming sites. A spam filter analyzes the e-mails themselves looking for words that spammers are likely to use.

Spammers are tricky and will sometimes stick random words into their messages hoping to evade filters. These "word salads" try to put the words that might be caught in the filter in between other words.

Some people routinely respond to spam, hoping to spam the spammers and clog up their e-mail boxes, but a better and safer course of action is to forward "unwanted or deceptive spam" to spam@uce.gov at the Federal Trade Commission. The database of collected spam is used to prosecute perpetrators of scam or deceptive advertising.

Fixing the Problem

Once you realize you have a sick computer, don't delay in cleaning it up. The more time a virus has, the more damage it can do. Remember that it could be e-mailing all of your friends and getting into their computers. It might be burrowing like a worm into your programs, destroying them. Or if it is a "time bomb," it will just sit and wait to activate itself.

Once a computer has caught a virus, you have a few options. Windows, for instance, allows you to perform an action called system restore, which is sort of like a time machine for your computer. You can return it to a time prior to the infection. Also, your virus software may be able to quarantine or remove the virus.

As a last-ditch effort, if a virus is on your system and antiviral software can't clean it and you can't solve your problem any other way, you may have to reinstall the operating system. This is a radical step that means erasing your entire hard drive and reinstalling the operating system from an uninfected source.

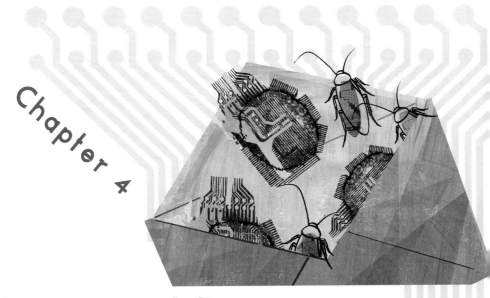

Viruses and Spam in the Real World

The hackers who create malicious computer viruses often view themselves as modern-day pirates. Usually they are extremely bright, but often times they are also isolated loner types who prefer their computers to other people. Statistically they are males who spend much of their time sitting in front of a computer.

There are three kinds of hackers: "white hat," "gray hat," and "black hat." The white hat hackers are people who try to use their hacking skill to prevent viruses and fix computer problems. Gray hat hackers are only interested in the game of hacking and don't care to either help or harm. And like the villains in Westerns, the black hat hackers are determined to cause trouble either for pleasure or for personal gain. The "good" hackers love computers and many of them would

Hackers and computer scientists combine forces to share their knowledge at the annual Hack in the Box Security Conference.

never dream of causing actual damage to them. Often hackers see themselves as outlaws and nonconformists, like Robin Hood or Jesse James.

According to the *LA Times*, during his trial, when famous hacker Kevin Mitnick was accused in court of harming a computer, his eyes welled up with tears. It was not the accusation of breaking into a corporate computer network that upset him so much as the idea that he would want to harm a computer. Mitnick used the term "social engineering" to describe his hacking experiments.

Mitnick is a hero to some who feel he was unfairly prosecuted. Imprisoned for five years in the late 1990s, he was temporarily locked in solitary confinement because the judge and jailers were afraid of his ability to manipulate technology. Upon his release, he was ordered not to touch a computer for the rest of his life; however, that decree was eventually softened, and in 2003, he was permitted to use a computer again. He now runs a company dedicated to helping stop harmful hackers.

The Elk Cloner, the first virus to appear "in the wild," or outside of the system where it was created, was written by fifteen-year-old Rich Skrenta. On the fiftieth booting up of the game Skrenta gave to his friends, this message appeared on the screen:

Elk Cloner: The program with a personality

It will get on all your disks
It will infiltrate your chips
Yes it's Cloner!

It will stick to you like glue
It will modify RAM too
Send in the Cloner!

Robert Morris was a grad student just playing around when he inadvertently released a worm "into the wild" in 1988. He is now a professor and software entrepreneur.

The Brain Virus

Basit and Amjad Farooq Alvi, owners of a computer store in Lahore, Pakistan, were twenty-six and nineteen years old respectively when they created the Brain virus and implanted it on every piece of software they sold. Their store was frequented by travelers, students, and others who brought the virus with them around the world. For the most part, little damage resulted, although the virus may have provided inspiration for less benign hackers.

The Morris Worm

The Morris Internet worm was created by Cornell University Ph.D. student Robert Morris in 1988. It quickly found its way into computer systems throughout the country. Morris had wanted to spread a harmless worm from computer to computer, but his code was flawed. The Internet worm copied itself so many times that it clogged up the Internet.

Morris soon realized what was happening and tried to send out instructions on how to remove the worm, but it was too late. The United States General Accounting Office estimated the damages at between $100,000 and $10 million to the six thousand systems infected nationwide. Morris was eventually sentenced to three years of probation and four hundred hours of community service and was fined $10,050.

Different Kinds of Viruses

So many different kinds of viruses exist and are being developed that it's impossible to make a complete list, but

Myths and Facts

Myth: As long as you don't give out your password, you're safe from hackers.

Fact: There are hundreds of common words that are most often used as passwords. Hackers can find their way into 90 percent of networks because chances are someone has used one of these words.

Myth: Only bad guys use disposable e-mail addresses.

Fact: It's a good idea for everyone to have a disposable e-mail address to use for surfing. Since you can easily get an address from Gmail, Yahoo!, or other providers, set up a secondary address that you give out to strangers.

Myth: Responding to spam is a way to get spammers to stop sending it.

Fact: It's better not to get involved with spammers at all. Although some people think that by beating them at their own game they can triumph, the most sensible thing is simply to report spam.

here are some of the most common viruses and some of their characteristics.

Macro Viruses

A macro virus is written in the scripting languages of such programs as Word and Excel and spreads by infecting documents and spreadsheets. Since macro viruses are written in the language of the application and not in that of the operating system, they are called platform dependent, which means they need a program in order to spread.

Logic Bombs

A logic bomb sits in your computer doing nothing until something triggers it. Sometimes deleting a file or printing a message will activate the virus. Time bombs are like logic bombs but their trigger is a specific time. The Jerusalem, or Friday the Thirteenth, virus was a time bomb.

Sentinels

A sentinel is a very advanced virus that allows its creator to take control of infected computers. The computers then become "zombie" or "slave" computers. Vast numbers of zombies can be used to launch a DOS, or denial of service attack. A DOS simply sends enough "zombie" e-mails to a Web site, blog, or discussion forum to effectively shut it down by clogging it with repetitive garbage.

Different Kinds of Spam

Phishing is a high-tech scam that uses spam or pop-up messages to trick you into giving out personal information like your credit card number, bank account information, Social Security number, and passwords. Phishing scams usually pretend that they are coming from a business or organization that you deal with, such as your bank, Paypal, or eBay, or even from the government. The message asks you to "update" or "validate" your account information. Many times it will claim that your account will be closed if you don't respond immediately.

You may also receive an e-mail generally marked "urgent" or "confidential" from someone asking for your help in moving "millions of dollars" out of their country. The scammer often claims to be a foreign bank manager, government official, the wife of a deceased general, or other important person who needs your help. Many times a spammer will offer you a "vast sum of money" for your help moving the money out of the country in the form of a forgotten account, diamonds or gold, a frozen inheritance, oil money, charity money, etc. The spammer will ask you for some kind of advance fee or for your bank account information.

If you receive an e-mail marked "Congratulations!" or "Confidential," which tells you you've won a lottery that you never entered, you can be sure you are a target of criminal spam.

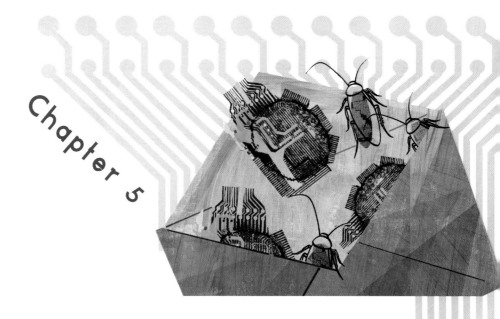

Chapter 5

Looking into the Future

In 2004, Microsoft chairman Bill Gates predicted that there would be no computer viruses left by 2006. If one of the world's richest men and most famous computer guys could be so very wrong, what can the rest of us expect to know?

At the same time as Gates predicted the end to malware, others suggested that a computer virus could elect the president of the United States. Hackers talk about changing traffic light patterns, phone numbers, tax records and banking and credit card information. Articles online and in magazines talk about how easy it would be to hack the IRS or the FBI.

The first wave of hackers were people who saw their actions in a more idealistic light than most others. Since the first bad viruses were released into the wild, hackers have attempted to create good viruses to fight back. There are a

Bill Gates, who predicted the end of spam by 2006, reportedly receives four million spam messages a day.

number of reasons why most people think that good viruses won't work. And while this is just the kind of challenge that appeals to hackers, remember that the first virus, Creeper, had an enemy named Reeper. The idea of every virus having an equal and opposite antivirus is about as old as viruses themselves.

Most people don't really think much of the idea for a number of reasons. As the Morris worm taught us, even "good" viruses don't always act the way they are supposed to. And no matter what the creator of the virus intends, it still trespasses on someone's computer, taking up precious disk space.

Legislation

In 2003, the federal government stepped in to create laws to limit spammers. The Can-Spam Act however didn't please computer users, who saw it as actually encouraging spam. The Federal Trade Commission also launched a public-relations

To create virus protection software, programmers have to understand how the virus works. This screen displays the code of a virus.

campaign to encourage e-mail users to simply never respond to a spam e-mail—ever.

In 2005, IBM announced a service to bounce spam directly to the computers that send out spam. Because the spammers' addresses are identified in the headers of every message, the computer sending the spam is easy to locate. But since most of these addresses are actually zombies, this doesn't really help much.

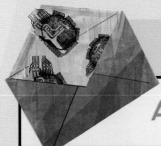

A Sampling of Spam

Subject Line: ILOVEYOU
Message Body: kindly check the attached LOVELETTER coming from me.

Subject Line: fwd: Joke
Message Body: empty

Subject Line: Mother's Day Order Confirmation
Message Body: We have proceeded to charge your credit card for the amount of $326.92 for the mother's day diamond special. We have attached a detailed invoice to this e-mail. Please print out the attachment and keep it in a safe place. Thanks Again and Have a Happy Mother's Day! mothersday@subdimension.com

Subject Line: Dangerous Virus Warning
Message Body: There is a dangerous virus circulating. Please click attached picture to view it and learn to avoid it.

Subject Line: Important! Read carefully!
Message Body: Check the attached IMPORTANT coming from me!

Subject Line: How to protect yourself from the ILOVEYOU bug!
Message Body: Here's the easy way to fix the love virus.

Subject Line: I Can't Believe This!!!
Message Body: I Can't Believe I have Just received This Hate E-mail . . . Take A Look!

Subject Line: Thank You For Flying With Arab Airlines
Message Body: Please check if the bill is correct, by opening the attached file.

Subject Line: Variant Test
Message Body: This is a variant to the vbs virus.

Subject Line: Yeah, Yeah another time to DEATH . . .
Message Body: This is the Killer for VBS.LOVE-LETTER.WORM.

Subject Line: LOOK!
Message Body: hehe . . . check this out.

Another response to spam has been to leave messages at the spammers' sites. The theory is that if even a tiny percentage of users visit spam sites just to leave negative messages, these messages would require that the spammers sort them out, and it would cost them money. A service called Blue Frog filled out the Web forms on these sites. Since half a million users subscribed to Blue Frog the volume could have disabled a site. However, Blue Frog was sued by a spammer and went out of business.

Spamming attacks inspired by disagreements between countries have included Arab and Israeli hackers attacking each other's Web sites and Pakistani versus Indian hackers. During the 2002 Olympics, when officials disqualified a South Korean speed skater who had bumped into an American skater, strikes that appeared to come from South Korea hit U.S. computers.

Spam and viruses aren't simply annoying to individuals. Some people fear for democracy itself. In Estonia in April of 2007, the government and businesses were beset by masses of e-mail. According to a spokesman for the government, the e-mails emerged from Russians angered at the relocation of a World War II memorial dedicated to Soviet soldiers. Although Estonians of Russian descent did riot in the streets, the majority of the damage occurred online due to malicious spam. This action was called "cyberwar" and marked the first time that such an attack gained worldwide attention.

Even as the government and private agencies attempt to control viruses and spam, new versions spring up daily. Since there is no way the world will stop using computers and since so much that is good about computers involves making contact, it's not likely or practical to stop using the Internet entirely.

Just as when you walk down the street in the real world you have to be careful to obey the walk/don't walk signs, you need to watch out for potholes, mean dogs, and other threats both big and small. You have to keep your eyes open when you use your computer, too. It's easy to forget when you are sitting in the comfort of your own home in your pajamas that you are also in a public space, but you need to remember that you don't know who else is there with you. Ideally, good will outweigh the dangers, and the best way for this to happen is for you to be smart and careful as you enjoy the remarkable things that the Internet offers.

Glossary

encryption The protecting of data in order to make it difficult to replicate, understand, or interpret.

firewall A digital barrier to prevent information from entering a computer. The firewall examines incoming data and rejects it if it does not seem safe.

floppy disk A small disk used to store and transfer files.

hacker Someone who manipulates computer software and technology.

in the wild A phrase used to describe a virus that travels beyond the network or laboratory where it was created.

logic bomb A type of virus that executes only when certain computer processes occur, such as the fiftieth launching of a file or when a certain word is typed.

malware Any kind of malicious software including viruses, Trojan horses, and worms.

network Two or more computers connected so that they can share files and/or equipment such as a printer.

stealth virus A virus that hides from antivirus software.

Trojan horse A malicious program that disguises itself as a harmless or helpful application.

virus A program that can spread from computer to computer by piggybacking itself to other programs.

worm A parasitic computer program that replicates, but unlike viruses, does not infect other computer program files.

zombie A computer that has been taken over by a virus and obeys the commands of an outside user.

For More Information

Canadian Broadcasting Corporation (CBC)
Audience Relations
P.O. Box 500, Station A
Toronto, ON M5W 1E6
Canada
Web site: http://www.cbc.ca
> Canada's broadcasting association's Web page has a section on technology with the latest news on computer viruses and worms as well as other technologically oriented stories.

Coalition Against Unsolicited Commercial E-mail (CAUCE)
CAUCE North America, Inc.
P.O. Box 727
Trumansburg, NY 14886
(303) 800 6345
E-mail: comments@cauce.org
Web site: http://www.cauce.org
> Formed in March of 2007, CAUCE is a North American organization devoted to the enforcement of antispam laws.

Computer Security Resource Center
NIST Computer Security Division
100 Bureau Drive
Mail Stop 8930
Gaithersburg, MD 20899-8930
(301) 975-8443
Web site: http://csrc.nist.gov
> A governmental organization whose mission is to increase computer security through awareness and research.

Security Focus Symantec Corporation
Suite 1000
100 4th Avenue SW
Calgary, AB T2P 3N2
Canada
(403) 261-5400
Web site: http://www.securityfocus.com/infocus/1286
   The Web site of this private company specializing in computer security
   provides a history of viruses as well as news about current threats.

Web Sites

Due to the changing nature of Internet links, Rosen Publishing
has developed an online list of Web sites related to the subject of
this book. This site is updated regularly. Please use this link to
access the list:

http://www.rosenlinks.com/cccs/visp

For Further Reading

Graham, Steve H. *The Good, the Spam and the Ugly*. New York, NY: Citadel, 2007.

Gralla, Preston. *Online Kids: A Young Surfer's Guide to Cyberspace*. New York, NY: John Wiley & Sons, 1999.

Henderson, Harry. *The Lucent Library of Science and Technology: Computer Viruses*. New York, NY: Lucent Books, 2005.

Rothman, Kevin F. *Coping with Dangers on the Internet: A Teen's Guide to Staying Safe Online*. New York, NY: The Rosen Publishing Group, 2000.

Willard, Nancy E. *Cyber-Safe Kids, Cyber-Savvy Teens: Helping Young People Learn to Use the Internet Safely and Responsibly*. New York, NY: Jossey-Bass, 2007.

Bibliography

Goodman, Danny. *Spam Wars: Our Last Best Chance to Defeat Spammers, Scammers & Hackers.* New York, NY: Select Books, 2004.

Jennings, Charles, and Lori Fena. *The Hundredth Window: Protecting Your Privacy and Security in the Age of the Internet.* New York, NY: John Wiley & Sons, 2003.

McAfee, John, and Colin Haynes. *Computers Viruses, Worms, Data Diddlers, Killer Programs, and Other Threats to Your System.* New York, NY: St. Martin's Press, 1989.

Mitnick, Kevin D., and William L. Simon. *The Art of Deception: Controlling the Human Element of Security.* New York, NY: John Wiley & Sons, 2002.

Index